Bryce Canyon National Park Tour Guide Book

By Waypoint Tours®

Front Cover - Bryce Canyon Hoodoos

Back Cover - Bryce Canyon Ampitheater in Winter by Ron Warner

Contents

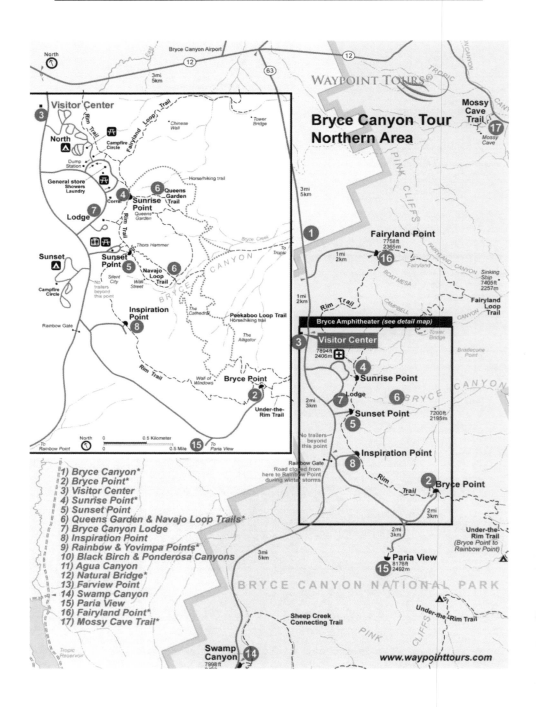

Bryce Canyon Tour Northern Area

1) Bryce Canyon*
2) Bryce Point*
3) Visitor Center
4) Sunrise Point*
5) Sunset Point
6) Queens Garden & Navajo Loop Trails*
7) Bryce Canyon Lodge
8) Inspiration Point
9) Rainbow & Yovimpa Points*
10) Black Birch & Ponderosa Canyons
11) Agua Canyon
12) Natural Bridge*
13) Farview Point
14) Swamp Canyon
15) Paria View
16) Fairyland Point*
17) Mossy Cave Trail*

www.waypointtours.com

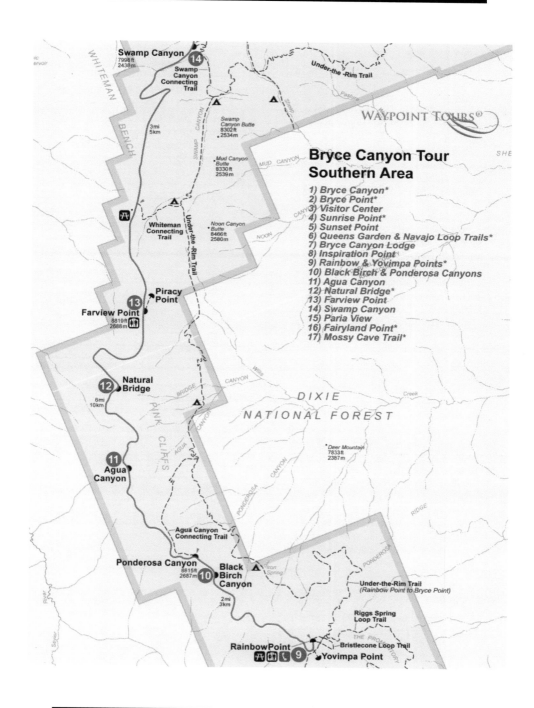

Bryce Canyon Tour
Southern Area

1) Bryce Canyon*
2) Bryce Point*
3) Visitor Center
4) Sunrise Point*
5) Sunset Point
6) Queens Garden & Navajo Loop Trails*
7) Bryce Canyon Lodge
8) Inspiration Point
9) Rainbow & Yovimpa Points*
10) Black Birch & Ponderosa Canyons
11) Agua Canyon
12) Natural Bridge*
13) Farview Point
14) Swamp Canyon
15) Paria View
16) Fairyland Point*
17) Mossy Cave Trail*

1) Bryce Canyon

What does a Mormon shipwright have in common with a wildlife menagerie nestled among enthralling geology adorned with a star-encrusted night sky? Answer: Bryce and the five years he was here. Welcome to Bryce Canyon National Park, named after shipwright Ebenezer Bryce. From the flame-colored spires beneath the rim, to the sparkling diamonds in the night sky, we hope you enjoy the magical beauty of Bryce Canyon.

Ebenezer Bryce was born in Dunblane, Scotland in 1830. As a shipwright's apprentice, he learned carpentry, the trade that would become his life. Bryce converted to the Church of Jesus Christ of Latter Day Saints and immigrated to the United States at the age of 17. Upon arriving in Utah, Bryce wed Mary Parker, and at the direction of the Mormon Church, the couple became serial homesteaders, going wherever the skills of a carpenter were most needed. They also managed to raise 12 children along the way! It was between 1875 and 1880 that the Bryces lived in the lower canyon.

By logging the flanks and irrigating the floor of the canyon that his neighbors christened with his name, Ebenezer supplied the fledging community with wood and water. It is unclear to what extent Bryce appreciated the world wonder that would immortalize his name. His only enduring quote about this rock labyrinth expresses more pragmatism than awe: "It's a hell of place to lose a cow."

The beauty of Bryce Canyon was not lost upon J.W. Humphrey who was the forest supervisor of lands that would eventually be united as the Dixie National Forest. Starting in 1916, he lobbied aggressively, sometimes even under an assumed name, to have the most scenic portion of his national forest bestowed with more protection than his agency could offer.

Step one occurred in 1923 when Bryce Canyon National Monument was established under the administration of the U.S. Forest Service. The following year saw it renamed as Utah National Park and transferred to the National Park Service. In 1928, a significant boundary expansion restored the name to Bryce Canyon National Park.

The primary reason for establishing the park was to protect and better understand the bizarre and beautiful geologic spires that would eventually be named "hoodoos", from the verb "hoodoo" meaning "to cast a spell". Later, as over-grazing, predator extermination, and pest poisoning took their toll on the surrounding region, Bryce also became a small but critical refuge for scores of animal species, including everything from the elusive mountain lion, to the highly endangered Utah prairie dog. Now, as the new and underestimated threat of light pollution spreads globally, Bryce Canyon's park rangers use this last small sanctuary of natural darkness as a platform from which to champion the fragile beauty of the night sky.

Indeed, where Ebenezer Bryce was worried about losing his cows among the hoodoos, many now come to Bryce with the intent of getting a little lost themselves in its beauty. As Park Ranger Kevin Poe puts it, "There's no question that the rocks are enchanting, but it's also a hell of a place to lose yourself ... among the stars."

2) Bryce Point

One of the most magical experiences you can have at Bryce Canyon is a sunrise at Bryce Point. Bryce Point, a tongue of the canyon's rim reminiscent of a ski jump, juts out into Bryce Amphitheater. As the sun rises in the east, its first light catches the tallest hoodoos, crawling downward, chasing away shadows. With every passing minute, dozens more are lit, like so many candles, until the entire basin is ablaze with orange and yellow light.

For some, the beauty needs no explanation. For others, it is impossible to gaze upon something so unique and not ask, "How?!" Although the rock story of Bryce is so complicated that even professors of geology can get temporarily lost in its intricacies, each reference to geology is presented as a puzzle piece, from which you can build the interlocking big picture.

Bryce's castle-like spires are predominately limestone, and not sandstone as many incorrectly assume. Rivers deposited dissolved calcium carbonate into the large, ancient Lake Claron. The lake lacked an out-flowing river to regulate the concentration of the dissolved lime. Just as water in northern Utah's Great Salt Lake can only escape by evaporation—making the remaining water ever saltier—so did this ancient lake become ever "limier". Eventually, the saturation point was overcome and limestone mud began to precipitate out of the water, filling the bottom of the lake.

Some geologists believe the uplift of the Colorado Plateau caused this lake to turn wrong-side-out, reversing the flow of the ancestral Colorado River. Instead of the Little Colorado flowing from southern Arizona into Lake Claron, the new Colorado River did an about face, breaking through to the Pacific Ocean, draining Lake Claron, and carving the Grand Canyon. The thousand-foot deep limestone mud flat left behind in Lake Claron's basin turned to stone, becoming the colorful Claron limestone layer that Bryce's so called canyons are now eroding into.

Do you see the "grottos" in the side wall of the canyon nook created by Bryce Point? Here in the ancient lake some sand WAS washed in, but because the sandstone erodes more easily in this climate than the limestone, it eroded away preferentially, leaving the cave-like pockets.

Three hiking trails depart from Bryce Point. The easiest is the Rim Trail, which follows the rim five-and-a-half miles north to Fairyland Point. From the parking lot, the five-and-a-half mile Peekaboo Loop descends steeply into the heart of Bryce Amphitheater. For backpackers, there's the 23-mile long Under-the-Rim Trail to the southern tip of the park. ALL hikers are cautioned to carry an approved map so they don't end up like Ebenezer's cows—lost among the hoodoos!

Page 11 - Bryce Amphitheater Sunrise &
Snowy Bryce Point
Page 12 - Bryce Point, Navajo Mountain
plus Fog & Cave-like Grottos

3) Bryce Canyon Visitor Center

The Visitor Center is located beside the entrance fee station. Here, friendly and knowledgeable park rangers can help you plan your visit, relay current weather information, and most importantly, provide you with a schedule of Bryce Canyon's compelling and entertaining ranger programs. Those traveling with kids will want to pick up a Bryce Canyon Junior Ranger Activity Booklet, heralded by the National Park Service's Chief of Interpretation as "one of the very best in the entire service."

Another must is the 22-minute version of the park's award winning film, "Shadows of Time." The Visitor Center elaborates on the film's themes of geology, ecology, history, and astronomy with many excellent exhibits that may help you identify some of the animals and flowers seen along Bryce's trails as well as better understand Bryce's geology and history. During the summer, the Visitor Center is also where volunteer astronomers will give you a close-up view of our sun through specially designed solar telescopes.

Finally, the Visitor Center is the key node of the Bryce Canyon Shuttle, which runs May to September. Although the Bryce Shuttle is optional, it's an efficient way to explore the most scenic and busiest sections of the park. One of the advantages of the shuttle is should you decide to hike one of the rim trails, you can hike just in one direction and not worry about how you're going to get back to your car! It also follows a long tradition of guided tours in the national parks, including the "white touring cars" used in the Utah National Parks from the 1920's until the outbreak of WWII. Hired locally, the friendly shuttle drivers know the park like the backs of their hands and exemplify their company's eager-to-please motto, "Ride with us! We'll watch the road so you can see the park!"

4) Sunrise Point

Sunrise Point is one of the best places to get a feel for the dynamic geology of Bryce. Do you see the Sinking Ship formation in the distance? Starting about 15 million years ago, the Paunsaugunt plateau has been lifted along the Paunsaugunt fault. Periodic earthquakes shifted blocks of earth along the fault, causing relatively rapid changes in the rock layer structures and creating the fractures which would eventually contribute to the unique hoodoos formations at Bryce. Sinking Ship was a block of rock whose left hand side "sank" relative to the right, and is now immortalized as one of Bryce's more easily recognized landscapes.

At Sunrise Point you can also easily observe how fast Bryce Canyon is eroding. Technically, Bryce is not a REAL canyon at all, because none of it is carved primarily by flowing water. Bryce Canyon is so unique that no name exists to define what it truly is. Therefore, accurate descriptions quickly become a mouthful, but they are worth mentioning. Consider how much meaning is lost by shortening "a-series-of-arroyo-shaped-amphitheaters-being-frost-wedged-into-the-edge-of-a-limestone-plateau" to simply "canyon!"

At Bryce, the extraordinary combination of a multitude of otherwise ordinary conditions cause frost wedging to be the primary force for both the weathering and the erosion of the rock. Two hundred days a year - winters are long at Bryce - the temperature soars above freezing during the afternoon, only to plummet back below freezing at night. All this freezing and thawing causes melting snow and ice to seep deeper into the heavily-fractured limestone by day, only to refreeze at night, wedging the cracks ever-wider until eventually chunks of rock fall.

Limestone eventually dissolves into clay which thickly coats the debris slopes under hoodoos and cliff walls. This clay, when saturated with melting snow, also swells and slumps with the daily freeze/thaw cycles, carrying all larger debris downhill like a conveyor belt.

How fast does all this geology happen? Unlike most places, at Bryce, the continual changes to the local geology can be documented within a human lifespan. On the west end of the fenced overlook, you might notice what could be mistaken for a sapling standing on bare roots, as if partially pulled from the ground by some malevolent but lazy giant. In actuality, this young limber pine is nearly 100 years old. So to answer the question, by comparing the tree's age to the four feet of rock and soil that has eroded out from under its roots, we can tell that Bryce Canyon's rim is eroding farther and farther west at a rate of one to four feet per 100 years!

Below - Sinking Ship plus Table Cliff Plateau
Page 16 - Limber Pine & Bryce Canyon in Fog

5) Sunset Point

While Sunset Point is many things, it is not the best place in the park to see a sunset. Indeed, there are few places in Bryce that are good for sunsets, because all of the park's amphitheaters face east and therefore become filled with shadow as sunset approaches. Instead, serious sunset photographers follow the setting sun 10 miles west on Highway 12 to the Dixie National Forest's Red Canyon. Here again, you will find amphitheaters cut into the beautiful Claron limestone, only these open to the west.

Sunset Point is the most popular overlook in the park and hiking opportunities abound here as well. For a leisurely, one mile round trip stroll, go north along the Rim Trail to Sunrise Point and back. Alternatively, the most beautiful section of the Rim Trail, known as the Silent City, lies to the south as part of a 1.5 mile round trip hike to Inspiration Point.

Page 19 - Snowy Sinking Ship plus Table Cliff Plateau & Juliet's Window

Directly below your feet is the Navajo Loop Trail, a favorite of the slot canyon fanatics as each side of the 1.3 mile loop has places where one can almost touch both walls from the trail. Don't let the short distance deceive you; the steepness of this trail makes it anything but easy. People love slot canyons, but the important thing to remember is that in southern Utah, slot canyons are commonplace.

There is, however, only one place in the world where you can walk among so many tall rock spires as if you were an ant on a pincushion, and that is the Queens Garden Trail. So, if you want the best of both worlds, combine the two into a larger 2.9 mile loop.

From Sunset Point you'll see that Bryce's Claron limestone comes in many colors. In its purest form, limestone is chalky white, as you can see in the highest portions of the cliffs. Mineral impurities can easily change the rock's color. Various forms of iron take credit for the reds, oranges, yellow, and even lime green, while manganese is responsible for the pinks and purples. Now add brilliant blue sky and puffy white clouds and Bryce Canyon presents a canvas of color like no other.

6) Queens Garden & Navajo Loop Trails

The most scenic way to hike the Queens Garden and Navajo Loop Combination Trail is to start at Sunset Point and go clockwise or north along the rim to begin your beneath-the-rim adventure with the Queens Garden Trail and finish with the Wall Street side of Navajo Loop. That way, the Queens Garden will unfold in front of you as you descend into it.

As you hike along the rim between Sunset and Sunrise Points, you may be able to spy segments of the trail below, winding among hoodoos, through tunnels, and in and out of canyons. You are not only about to hike the best three mile hike at Bryce - it's possible that it's the best three mile hike anywhere!

A common question while hiking the Queens Garden is, "What's the name of that hoodoo?" The simple answer is, "Whatever you want it to be!" In the early years, the National Park Service named dozens of hoodoos, but because many of these no longer stand, the names have also been allowed to erode.

Queen Victoria, the namesake of the region and this trail, is one proud exception. She stands off the main trail on a short spur. Though not as large as the surrounding hoodoos, it is remarkable in that it looks like a queen from all possible angles.

After returning to the main trail, continue downhill until you arrive at the junction of the Navajo Loop. Downhill and to your left are 3.5 extra miles known as the Peekaboo Loop. Alternatively, going to the right or straight ahead will put you in one of the slot canyons of the Navajo Loop, and after a short but steep climb, you'll be back where you started at Sunset Point. If much more is revealed, you'll lose out on the thrill of self discovery. Either way, the best is yet to come; but if you want a little hint, continue straight ahead through Wall Street.

Below - Queen Victoria Hoodoo
Page 23 - Wall Street

QUEENS GARDEN
END OF TRAIL
TO NAVAJO LOOP
SUNSET POINT 1.4 MI

7) *Bryce Canyon Lodge*

Hidden among the ponderosa pines, Ruby and Minnie Syrett built "Tourist's Rest" to accommodate the hundreds of visitors who began to hear about Bryce's magical beauty in the early 1900's. The Union Pacific Railroad bought Tourist's Rest and replaced it with the Bryce Canyon Lodge. Its architect, Gilbert Stanley Underwood, is most famous for his masterpieces, the Ahwahnee in Yosemite National Park in 1927, and the Jackson Lake Lodge in Grand Teton in 1954. Of slightly lesser acclaim, are Underwood's lodges on the Colorado Plateau including the Bryce and Zion Lodges in 1925, and the Grand Canyon Lodge at the North Rim in 1928. Of these three, only the Bryce Canyon Lodge remains. The other two perished in flames and reconstructed approximations now stand in their places.

As grand and powerful as Underwood's designs were, he also went to great lengths to make sure the buildings didn't compete with the grandeur of the national parks in which they resided. This is why the Bryce Canyon Lodge is hidden among the pines and positioned back away from the rim. The wavy pattern of the roofs is another famous design element that helps hide the lodges in the forest. In actuality, the roofs are perfectly flat, but you won't be able to convince your eyes of this because of the optical illusion created by uniquely cutting each shingle.

The Bryce Canyon Lodge offers fine dining, rustic rooms, cozy cabins, a gift shop, horseback rides into the canyon, and nightly ranger programs. In summary, it's a rare opportunity to immerse yourself in a bygone era. It's worth a look - especially if you are seeking shelter from a lightning storm.

Statistically, Bryce Canyon is one of the most dangerous National Parks for lightning. Bryce's thunderstorms arrive suddenly and are horrifically powerful, pounding the rim with multiple bolts every minute. Retreating to a car greatly reduces your risk, but buildings offer the best protection. If you cannot reach either form of hard cover, crouch in a low spot, or better yet, hunker down beside a large rock or fallen log. Do not, under any circumstances, take refuge under a standing tree, because lightning is most likely to strike tall, isolated objects. Waiting out a storm may mean seeing less of Bryce than you had hoped for, but it will also insure that you have the opportunity to visit Bryce again!

8) Inspiration Point

The top of Inspiration Point gives you a commanding view of Bryce Amphitheater, and you may feel a kindred spirit with the Violet-green swallows or White-throated swifts soaring over the hoodoos below. You can tell a violet-green swallow from the white-throated swift by its white belly. The swift has a white and black belly, and in flight, it may appear to be alternating the flapping of its wings. Actually, the swift beats one wing faster than the other in order to steer itself during flight because its tail is too short to act as a real rudder. It must not be too much of a handicap, as the White-throated swifts may be among the fastest birds, traveling over 100 miles per hour.

If you are already having a hard time adjusting to Bryce Canyon's high altitude, however, you may prefer to settle for the views from one of the two lower overlooks.

The Rim Trail along Inspiration Point is narrow with steep side-slopes. Vegetation on these slopes is sparse and the soil is treacherously loose. Stay on the trail and leave the slopes to the chipmunks and lizards. Because of cold nighttime temperatures, Bryce Canyon has few reptiles. However, here you might spy Mountain Short-horned lizards, Western Fence lizards, and the colorful Side-blotched lizards. Of the three, the Mountain Short-horned lizard draws the most attention. These small, flat-bodied, short-tailed reptiles have the ability to change the color of their skin to communicate aggression and improve their camouflage. How do you find one? Look for their favorite meal: ants. If you wait beside an ant hill, you might see what at first looks like a tiny pile of gravel approaching.

The chasing or handling of lizards, as with all park animals, is illegal and certainly not worth the risk of leaving the safety of the trail. To put it simply, lose the trail and you're likely to lose your footing, and maybe even your life.

Below - Violet-Green Swallow
Page 27 - Upper Inspiration Point Overlook
& Bryce Amphitheater

9) Rainbow & Yovimpa Points

Now it's time to visit some of Bryce's more secret locations. The most systematic way to see the rest of the park is to drive directly to the southern end and stop at the rest of the overlooks on your way back. As you head south, you will notice the landscape changing as you gain altitude. The transition between life zones is expressed in many ways. Ponderosa pines give way to spruce and fir. Wild turkey and mule deer live among the pines, but in the spruce and fir forests, their equivalents are blue grouse and elk.

The 18-mile long scenic drive ends at a large parking lot that serves both Rainbow Point, which looks north, and Yovimpa Point, which looks south. From the railing at Rainbow Point, you can enjoy a view of the entirety of Bryce Canyon National Park stretching toward the northern horizon. If you follow the railing to the left, you'll be able to look down on one of the park's more famous hoodoos, "the poodle."

Many birders also come here to scan the sky, because Rainbow Point is occasionally frequented by California condors. Absent since Ebenezer Bryce's time, the nine foot wingspans of the condors once again cast enormous shadows on the cliffs of Bryce. In the early 1990's, experts predicted that the species would be lost forever, but now 20-30 of these captive-raised giants fly free here. Turkey vultures and golden eagles, though smaller, are often incorrectly reported as condors. However, you can be certain if you know what to look for. Because all condors wear wing bands, the saying goes, "If it's almost as big as an airplane, and has numbers on its wings like an airplane, it's either a condor... or an airplane."

Yovimpa Point offers one of the most expansive vistas available amid the landscape that 1880's geologist Clarence E. Dutton coined the Grand Staircase. Past the pink cliffs of Bryce Canyon etched in Claron limestone, notice the grey cliffs of Tropic shale, and the white cliffs of Navajo sandstone, and the vermillion cliffs of the Kayenta formation of Zion fame.

To a geologist, these broken rows of colored cliffs demarcate the thick pages of earth's detailed diary - a diary that records the explosion of multicellular life, insects' pioneering of the land, the transition between fish and amphibians, the rise and fall of dinosaurs, the triumph of birds, and the slow but supreme domination by mammals. Other copies of these geologic pages are found scattered around the world; but in most places, volcanoes, earthquakes, glaciers, and such have burned, crumpled, or shredded them so much they are difficult to read.

The Grand Staircase is unique in that almost all of the pages of earth history can be easily read within this one vast region that stretches from the Claron limestone beneath your feet, over the southern horizon, and downward into the very bowels of the Grand Canyon. This overlook displays not only a hundred miles of distance, but also a billion years of time.

Can you comprehend the enormity of a billion years? Maybe it's easier to start smaller. Can you envision a thousand years? Maybe Two? Some of the trees here might help.

In Nevada, bristlecone pines have been determined to be nearly 5,000 years old! Bryce's bristlecones are babies by comparison being only 1,000-1,800 years old. Nevertheless, if you hike the one mile Bristlecone Loop Trail between Yovimpa and Rainbow Point, try to put yourself in the shoes, or rather the roots, of these trees; maybe you'll find a way to better understand time on a different scale, without getting lost in its depths.

10) Black Birch & Ponderosa Canyons

As you return northward, the first overlooks you come to are Ponderosa and Black Birch Canyon. Confusingly, neither overlook has the tree species it is named for. The semantic trick is that hidden in the canyons far below are both water birch and ponderosa pines, colloquially known as black birch. The latter name arose to distinguish them from quaking aspen, which, though similar in appearance to paper birch, is a completely unrelated species. Whew! If you think tree nomenclature is confusing, it's not nearly as difficult as managing a diverse and healthy forest.

Much of the park's southern forest is dead or dying. These blue spruce trees have been attacked by the spruce bark beetle. Female beetles bore through the outer bark and lay hundreds of eggs in the inner bark – the life force of the tree. The eggs become ravenous larva that devours the tree from the inside out. When the larva mature into beetles, they fly to other trees, continuing the chain reaction of destruction.

A tree's only defense is to produce enough sap to flush the eggs out before they reach the larval stage. The reason this isn't working is because there's no longer enough water to go around. For the last hundred years the rainfall has remained more or less constant; however, the number of spruce living on a given acre has increased by a factor of ten. Now, each tree can produce only a tenth of the sap needed for defense against the bugs.

Had it been realized earlier that forest fires were not the enemy of forest health, but actually the prime regulators of ecological vigor, then the National Park Service would not have aggressively extinguished all fires and the unnaturally high density of spruce would have been avoided. A walk in these woods is reminiscent of Rachael Carson's *Silent Spring*. The birds are gone, terrestrial wildlife has abandoned the region, and even gusts of wind blowing through the dead twigs sound like sickly gasps.

But all hope is not lost. While correcting ecological mistakes is never easy, Bryce Canyon National Park Rangers are working hard and with scientific conviction to carefully reintroduce fire as a regenerative force. Prescribed fire continues to be a slow and controversial process, but recent successes indicate the next generation of park visitors will find the forests restored to their original glory.

11) Agua Canyon

In Spanish, agua means water. However, you won't find any water at Bryce's Agua Canyon unless it's raining. While rain at Zion can mean lethal flash floods, hikers at Bryce need not worry because the canyons of Bryce are at the very top of their watersheds, where the catchment basins are still small. However, once you're farther east in the Paria Canyons, flashfloods again become a serious danger.

Water is of extreme importance in the desert. The Paiute American Indians, who have inhabited this region since the Puebloan people deserted it 800 years ago, have a special connection to water. The syllable "Pa" occurs in a great many Paiute words. It can mean either water or spiritual power and sometimes both as in the name Paiute, which simultaneously means "people of the water" and "people of the power." Pa is most common in place names, where it often describes the location and/or quality of the water.

For example, the plateau you are standing on is called Paunsaugunt, which conceptually means "year round water is at the beaver ponds." Panguitch, referring to the largest natural lake in the region, means "water with big fish." Paria, referring to the river that cuts the deep canyons you see in the distance, means both "water with elk" and "water with mud."

The information conveyed epitomizes how water in the desert is a double-edged sword. During drought years, the Paria is the only source of water, so thirsty elk can be ambushed along its banks. However, when the normally sparkling water of this creek suddenly turns muddy, a 20-foot wall of water rolling rocks the size of SUVs is less than five minutes behind.

Perhaps it is in part due to this understanding of water that the Paiute thrived whereas the Publeoan cultures were lost. Sadly for the Paiute, during the 1800's, water took on a different definition of life and death with the arrival of Spanish ranchers and later, Mormon pioneers. These new Americans needed lots of water to keep their farms and livestock alive, and if necessary, they would fight for it.

12) Natural Bridge

Below you stands a thin wall of rock with a large beautiful hole in it that was not carved by humans. And that is about all that the landform authorities can agree upon.

Some argue that it can't be called a bridge, as natural bridges are carved by flowing water and water only flows here during heavy rain. Others, when told they can't call it a natural bridge, will default to the label "arch" and follow the classic distinction that arches are carved by wind.

Geologists retort that, "If your definition hinges on wind, then this can't be an arch because wind erosion doesn't happen at Bryce." They go on to explain that sandstone can be eroded by wind because even though sandstone has a hardness of 5, it weathers into sand grains which have a hardness of 6. Blow hardness of 6 against hardness of 5 and yes, it will make holes. However, Bryce's rock is limestone with a hardness of 4 which erodes into clay with a hardness of 1. Clay with a hardness of 1 could have been blowing against limestone with a hardness of 4 for millions of years and still never have made this hole.

Physicists thunder, "This is all nonsense! Natural holes are all caused by gravity. Who cares what process first weakens the rock? It's always gravity that makes it break and fall."

Bryce Canyon's park rangers explain that unlike most places with bridges or arches, here, frost wedging is the primary force acting upon the rock. In hopes of skirting the debate, they quickly continue that here all such holes, even though formed in similar manner to the potholes in your street, should just be called "windows."

Whereas an accumulation of potholes can degrade your streets and lower your property value, the widening of a window, to the point where the headpiece collapses, results in yet another unique landform.

It is the policy of the National Park Service to NOT prevent erosion from inevitably collapsing such wondrous windows. While this may seem somewhat callous, Bryce is really a celebration of broken holes in rock. We call the leftover standing legs - hoodoos! Hoodoos do not erupt from the ground like volcanoes, but instead are just the hardest remnants of broken windows. Accumulate enough hoodoos and you have a priceless treasure: Bryce.

13) Farview Point

This overlook named Farview Point is aptly named as Bryce Canyon has some of the cleanest and purest air left anywhere in the United States. From this waypoint, on an average day, you can make out the big blue dome of Navajo Mountain 80 miles away. On a good day, just to the right of Navajo Mountain, you can see a faint blue triangle barely discernable from the sky. This is the end of First Mesa on the Hopi Reservation in eastern Arizona, approximately 150 miles away. Wait until dark and then look next to the hind legs of the constellation Pegasus, and with your naked eye you'll be able to see the oval-shaped smudge that is the Andromeda Galaxy. Now you can see 2.6 million light years or approximately 15 quintillion miles. Now that's a far view!

Bryce Canyon's night sky is so dark you can see star clusters and galaxies with binoculars. Anywhere else a portable telescope would be needed. Most rural communities have a dark sky rating of 5.0 and offer 2,000 visible stars. Bryce's sky is rated at 7.4 and sparkles with over 7,500 stars.

When it comes to seeing stars, air quality is only part of the equation. Bryce is far from civilization and the unnecessary evil of light pollution. Here in this last grand sanctuary of natural darkness, Bryce's Astronomy Rangers, also known as Dark Rangers, will show you dazzling beauty you didn't realize had been lost, and will suggest how you can help recover some of that same beauty in your own hometown.

As much as the Dark Rangers love astronomy, they will be the first to tell you that there's more to be lost because of light pollution than just the hobby of telescope owners. Owls, amphibians, and most mammals require natural darkness to either hunt prey or hide from their predators. Plants determine the change of season by the number of hours of continuous darkness. Light pollution causes premature flowering in the spring and delayed winter dormancy in the fall. Darkness is also important for human health. Studies show that humans sleep best in darkness equivalent to a starry sky. Those who don't sleep well are at much higher risk to various forms of cancer. With all this in mind, maybe you should stay another night under Bryce's stars?

14) Swamp Canyon

When you stand at the Swamp Canyon Overlook, don't be disappointed if you can't see a swamp in all of this desert landscape. It's all about perspective. In a place where the rivers don't have to have water in them all the time to still be called rivers, a spring in a meadow might seem like a swamp. The spring in question is about two miles away and can be visited by hiking the 4.3 mile Swamp Canyon Loop. At the spring you could find tiger salamanders, desert spadefoot toads, and a couple of other species from Bryce's meager selection of amphibians.

This loop is popular among birders because it traverses four distinctly different habitats and thus offers the opportunity to see almost all of Bryce Canyon's 175 species of birds.

As with any portion of the park, the animals you are most likely to see are mule deer, common raven, Steller's jay, chipmunks, and golden-mantled ground squirrels which look like huge chipmunks. On this trail, you'll notice that all these animals have a little bit more respect for humans than elsewhere in the park. That is because the people who generally hike this more out-of-the-way trail are the true animal lovers who realize that while feeding animals might be immediately gratifying for the humans, it's actually an act of animal cruelty.

Before you think one potato chip won't hurt that little chipmunk, imagine how you'd feel after eating a potato chip the size of your whole body! What about four to five times a day, every day for six months? Fed animals congregate in parking lots where they are more likely to be killed by careless motorists. Fed animals teach their babies to beg instead of how to obtain their natural foods. When winter comes and the human handouts are no longer available, the whole animal family may die the slow agonizing death of starvation.

Be a true animal lover: keep your food to yourself and encourage others to do the same.

15) Paria View

While almost every overlook in the park is good for sunrise photography, few make for good sunsets. Paria View is the exception. If you scurried around this morning trying to get as many different sunrise pictures as possible, now you can relax. Here the sun will sink into a low spot on the ridge, and for a few magical moments, light the huge castle of rock in front of you like a scene from one of Peter Jackson's *Lord of the Rings* films.

Photographers aren't the only life forms that are most active during sunrise and sunset. The ecological term for this is "crepuscular" and it's an especially good way to live in desert-like environments. A perfect example is greenleaf manzanita -- the low, dense, red-barked evergreen shrubs found throughout the park.

Did you notice how all manzanita leaves point straight up? This is because they only do photosynthesis at sunrise and sunset when temperatures are lower and they won't lose as much precious water while taking in carbon dioxide. This is also the time to keep your eyes peeled for other crepuscular favorites that call Bryce Canyon home including deer, elk, coyotes, fox, black bear, and mountain lions.

The short spur road that leads to Paria View is not plowed in the winter to provide cross-country skiers a place to practice their sport when snow depths are too shallow to traverse the forests and meadows. When there is sufficient snowpack for off-trail exploration, one of the Bryce rangers' favorite snowshoe routes follows the hilly rim from here to Bryce Point, returning by looping back through the meadow. Now you have another reason, besides the splendor of snow-capped hoodoos, to entice you back for an off-season visit.

16) Fairyland Point

Bryce's magical beauty causes many, including the original Indian inhabitants themselves, to envision that giants and magical creatures have played a role in its formation. The 1800's explorer, Captain Clarence E. Dutton, wrote in his *Geology of the High Plateaus of Utah*:

"Standing obelisks, prostrate columns, shattered capitols, panels, niches, buttresses, repetitions of symmetrical forms, all bring vividly before the mind suggestions of the work of giant hands, a race of genii once rearing temples of rock, but now chained up in a spell of enchantment, while their structures are falling in ruins through centuries of decay."

Fairyland Point is located one mile north of the Visitor Center, and it is intentionally not signed in the southbound direction to improve traffic flow. For those who know Bryce well, this a favorite overlook because the hoodoos stand tall enough that you can look them in the eye.

This overlook is the northern terminus of the Rim Trail and part of the eight mile long Fairyland Loop Trail. Undoubtedly, the best time to hike this section of the park is in the spring, when the forests and meadows above the rim are exploding with the colors of a variety of wildflowers.

Several species and colors of paintbrush and penstemon are punctuated with blue flax, the white and purple petals of sego lilies, spiky red thistles, and the yellow and pink flowers of various species of cactus.

Surprised to hear of cactus growing alongside wildflowers? Surely by now you've come to realize that Bryce is a realm of blended ecological boundaries. Where else can a great horned owl dine on snowshoe hares, ringtails, skunk, and prairie dogs without having to fly more than a mile from its nest?

Because of the abundance of wildlife, the Fairyland Canyons are also where Bryce's Dark Rangers prefer to lead full moon hikes. Besides owls and bats, you may also be so lucky as to see rattlesnakes, the tree-climbing gray fox, fresh mountain lion tracks, and the beautiful and highly fragrant flowers of the bronze evening primrose which bloom for one night only. These highly acclaimed and very popular hikes are usually offered May through September, so make sure to call the Visitor Center well in advance for more information.

Below - Primrose
Page 42 - Great Horned Owl & Rattlesnake

17) Mossy Cave Trail

Water Canyon, also known for the half-mile long Mossy Cave Trail, is in the northern portion of Bryce Canyon off Highway 12. In the 1880's, Mormon pioneers used this canyon, in conjunction with a 10-mile long canal dug with hand tools, to divert water from the East Fork of the Sevier River across the plateau, through the divide, and eventually to what would become their new town of Tropic. Only during the drought of 2002 did the Tropic Ditch run dry.

After crossing the second footbridge, the trail forks. To the left is a short but steep climb to a shady overhang that's carpeted with moss during the summer, but choked with huge columns of ice in winter. The right hand trail dead ends overlooking a small waterfall. From this vantage point, you might realize just how wonderfully unique Bryce Canyon National Park really is.

In the formation at the top of the hill across from the waterfall, notice how some of the rock layers have eroded more readily than others. Dolomite, which has more magnesium than calcium, is more resistant to erosion than limestone and forms a "cap rock" for many of the unique formations seen in Bryce and even forms the lip of the waterfall seen below. But why are there fewer hoodoos in this section of the park? Why is this canyon more V-shaped? Why is there so much more vegetation?

The answer is that, unlike the other "canyons" in Bryce, this one has become a REAL canyon. No longer is frost-wedging the main erosive force. Like Zion Canyon, the Grand Canyon, and other canyons a million times over, Water Canyon is now being carved by flowing water. What a difference a little flowing water can make.

On the other hand, what a wonderfully unique landscape the lack of flowing water can make. By now you've had the opportunity to lose yourself for a while in the magic of Bryce Canyon National Park. What have you found? What images and experiences will you carry forward? Was it that sunrise from Bryce Point where the hoodoos burned with ruddy light as if aflame? Was it the lucky sighting of a mountain lion track that confirmed for you that truly wild places still exist? Was it the realization that no inheritance of diamonds could outshine the beauty of bequeathing your great-grandchildren with at least one place where they can always treasure a pristine starry sky? To many, Bryce has come to mean "magical beauty". What would Ebenezer, and his cows, have thought about that?

Page 44 Bottom - Icy Mossy Cave in Winter

18) Zion

Welcome to Zion, a land of sheer cliffs, ancient sand dunes, amazing vistas, and verdant garden alcoves.

How did Zion come to be named Zion? Pioneer Isaac Behunin, leafing through the Book of Isaiah one evening, was struck by the way the setting sun's last ruddy light hit Red Arch Mountain. The name came to him by epiphany as he skimmed through Isaiah chapter 2 verse 3: "And many people shall go and say, Come ye, and let us go up the mountain of the Lord ... and we will walk in his paths: for out of Zion shall go forth the law."

Mormon pioneers believed that Zion meant "sanctuary" and its rugged beauty was proof that God wanted them to settle there. However, in the early 1900's, visiting photographers, artists, and a surveyor named Leo Snow argued that Zion was far too beautiful to keep secret from the rest of the world. In 1909, President Howard Taft elevated Zion to national monument status under the Paiute name Mukuntuweap, meaning "straight canyon." However, like the Paiute American Indians themselves, the name, which had existed here for over 800 years, was already fading from the region. In 1919, when the United States Congress upgraded Mukuntuweap from monument to national park status, they renamed it "Zion" at the urging of the new Utahans.

Now about 2.5 million pilgrims from around the world are drawn here each year. Some come to gaze in awe at the majesty of Zion's grandeur with pedestals of stone so tall and massive they seem to support the sky. Rock climbers pit their muscle against these mighty walls, inching upward on ascents that can last days. Geologists work in the opposite direction. Descending the walls and tracking changes in the rock, they can almost travel back through time, learning how our planet works by understanding the changes it has undergone. Others come to celebrate the diversity of life housed here. Reminiscent of Eden, Zion sustains an impressive species list of 800 plants, 75 mammals, 271 birds, 32 reptiles and amphibians, and 6 native fish.

Zion is also nirvana for the hiker. The park's trails offer a full spectrum of hiking challenges. Following these paths can mean anything from a leisurely riverside stroll, to a multi-night backpack, to a white-knuckled, chain-assisted ascent over 1000 feet above the ground.

Zion is also a crown jewel of the National Park Service, a shining result of the dedication of men and women who strive to leave these works of nature clean, beautiful, and natural, for the enjoyment of future generations. As you begin your own Zion experience, be prepared as you will soon understand exactly the grandeur that overcame Isaac Behunin when he named this place, Zion.

19) Grand Canyon North Rim

One of the most common questions in Arizona is "Which side of the Grand Canyon is better, the South Rim or North Rim?" Like most comparative debates, this one is best answered with "It depends ... ". If cell coverage, IMAX theaters, warm temperatures, and proximity to interstates are a must, then the South Rim is for you. However, if you are looking to get away from the crowds and prefer conifers to cactus, the North Rim is your kind of paradise.

Getting to the North Rim is not easy. For most of the year, deep snow makes it inaccessible to all but the most athletic backcountry skiers. Even between late May and early October, the North Rim is fully three hours farther away from Las Vegas, Nevada or Phoenix, Arizona than the South Rim.

Perhaps it is the desert environment of the South Rim that makes the impression that the Grand Canyon is a calamity rather than a masterpiece. In the minds of the casual visitor, this South Rim perspective has always dominated. Looking up and across from the barren brink of the South Rim, classic descriptions like, "A gash in Nature's breast laid bare" seem accurate enough.

However, when looking down from the forested vantage of the North Rim, the Canyon's tremendous story of erosion looks less like devastation and more like craftsmanship.

Seeing the Grand Canyon as both a production and a destruction leads to a more enlightened understanding and appreciation of this world wonder. Indeed, just-a-big-hole-in-the-ground thinking is like accusing Michelangelo of defacing blocks of marble.

Theodore Roosevelt understood the canyon's duality. When proclaiming it a national monument in 1908, Roosevelt called it, "the most impressive piece of scenery I have ever looked at. It is beautiful and terrible and unearthly." Although Roosevelt spoke from the South Rim, if he were alive today, he would undoubtedly be a "north-rimmer". Speaking just as directly to untold future generations as he was the tourism developers in attendance, Roosevelt concluded his speech with a poignant caution, "Leave it as it is! You cannot improve upon it! The ages have been at work on it, and man can only mar it."

While a cynic, standing at the South Rim could grumble that Roosevelt's admonition was forgotten long ago, an optimist should take the cynic by the hand and say, "Roosevelt's Grand Canyon still exists! We just need to go to the North Rim." Welcome to the North Rim of Grand Canyon National Park!

20) Grand Canyon South Rim

Welcome to Grand Canyon National Park! As you approach the Grand Canyon, you are crossing the Colorado Plateau, a 130,000 square mile bulge in the earth's surface spanning half of Utah and a good portion of Arizona, New Mexico, and Colorado. Around its edges are the upthrust Rocky Mountains, the stretched-apart Great Basin, the contorted rocks of Arizona's Transition Zone, and ancient volcanoes. Despite all the geologic activity around it, the plateau has managed to stay relatively flat and unfolded, but as a whole, it may have been uplifted nearly two miles.

It is the uplift and the down cutting that have created the canyon. About five to six million years ago, the Colorado River began to carve its way down through the domed region on its way to the sea. Like a knife slicing through a layer cake, the mile-deep river canyon exposed multi-hued layers of time; a geologist's dream come true. However, you don't have to be a geologist to appreciate the canyon's grandeur.

Erosion by wind, water, and gravity not only widened the canyon, it created an amazing variety of towers and spires, ridges and side canyons, shadows and highlights. The rainbow of rock colors is most intense in early morning or late afternoon light. If you are lucky, you will see a storm chase through the canyon casting shadows and mist as it goes.

Sightseers have been coming to view the wonders of the canyon since 1883. Prospectors soon found tourism more profitable than mining and built accommodations for them. One of the earliest visitors was Theodore Roosevelt, a lover of the West's wide-open spaces. He pushed for federal protection and in 1893, the area became a Forest Reserve. In 1908, it received a promotion to National Monument and in 1919, the National Park was authorized by Congress. The most recent upgrade was in 1975 when its boundaries were expanded, doubling its size.

As you enter the park, you'll receive a copy of the park newspaper, The Guide, from the National Park Service, which is a great source of information on restaurants, lodging, parking, ranger talks, activities and other guest services within or near the park. It includes maps, hours, prices, and other helpful information.

Waypoint Tours®

Plan, Enhance & Cherish
Your Travel Adventures!

This Waypoint Tour® is your
personal tour guide unlocking the
fascinating highlights, history,
geology & nature of
Bryce Canyon National Park.

Waypoint Tours® are entertaining,
educational, self-guided tours to help
plan your travel adventures,
enhance your travel experience &
cherish your travel memories.

Travel Destinations include:
Bryce Canyon UT
Grand Canyon South Rim AZ
Grand Canyon North Rim AZ
Grand Teton WY
Mt. McKinley Denali AK
Rocky Mountains CO
San Antonio & Missions TX
San Diego CA
San Francisco CA
Sedona Red Rock Country AZ
Washington DC
Yellowstone WY
Yosemite CA
Zion UT

DVD & CD Complete Tour Packages
DVD Tour Guides
DVD Tour Postcards
MP3 Downloadable Audio Tours
GPS Waypoint Tours® for iPhones +
Tour Guide Books Plus DVD & MP3s
Tour Road Guides Plus Audio CDs
Tour Guide Books

Waypoint Tours® Available Online at:
www.waypointtours.com
www.amazon.com
www.itunes.com

Highlights, History, Geology,
Nature & More!

Credits

Book by Waypoint Tours®
Photography by Waypoint Tours®,
Ron Warner & Kevin Poe
Original Tour Script by Kevin Poe
Editing by Laurie Ann
Maps by the National Park Service

Support Bryce Canyon National Park
with a membership or donation to:

Bryce Canyon Natural History Assoc.
P.O. Box 640051
Bryce, Utah 84764
(435) 834-4782
http://www.brycecanyon.org

Bryce Canyon National Park
P.O. Box 640201
Bryce Canyon UT 84764
(435) 834-5322
http://www.nps.gov/brca

Photo Credits:
Back Cover, 7T, 8B, 9, 11TB, 12T,
16TB, 19TB, 22T, 27T, 34, 44B, 52,
53 by Ron Warner
Pages 3, 26, 38T, 42TB
by Kevin Poe
Pages 8T, 40 by the
National Park Service
T=Top, B=Bottom, R=Right, L=Left

Optional Audio CD Contents

Audio CD Driving Tour (62 min)

Optional DVD-ROM Contents

DVD Narrated Tour (36 min)
MP3 Audio Tour (62 min)
PC Multimedia Screensaver
Digital Photo Gallery

Breathtaking Photography,
Professional Narration &
Beautiful Orchestration

DVD Plays Worldwide in All Regions
DVD Mastered in HD in English
* Denotes Waypoints on DVD
PC Multimedia Screensaver &
Digital Photo Gallery Each Contain
40+ High-Resolution Photos

Professional Voicing by
Janet Ault & Mark Andrews
Recording Studio by Audiomakers
For private non-commercial use only
Detailed info & credits on
DVD-ROM

Optional Audio CD & DVD-ROM Info

Track #) Title

1) Bryce Canyon*
2) Bryce Point*
3) Visitor Center
4) Sunrise Point*
5) Sunset Point
6) Queens Garden &
   Navajo Loop Trails*
7) Bryce Canyon Lodge
8) Inspiration Point
9) Rainbow & Yovimpa Points*
10) Black Birch & Ponderosa Canyons
11) Agua Canyon
12) Natural Bridge*
13) Farview Point
14) Swamp Canyon
15) Paria View
16) Fairyland Point*
17) Mossy Cave Trail*
18) Zion*
19) Grand Canyon*

Leave No Trace

Made in the USA
Charleston, SC
03 October 2011